RELINQUENDA

THE NATIONAL POETRY SERIES

The National Poetry Series was founded in 1978 to
ensure the publication of five poetry books annually through
five participating publishers. Publication is funded annually
by the Lannan Foundation, Amazon Literary Partnership,
Barnes & Noble, the Poetry Foundation, the PG Family
Foundation and the Betsy Community Fund, Joan Bingham,
Mariana Cook, Stephen Graham, Juliet Lea Hillman Simonds,
William Kistler, Jeffrey Ravetch, Laura Baudo Sillerman,
and Margaret Thornton. For a complete listing of generous
contributors to the National Poetry Series, please visit
www.nationalpoetryseries.org.

2021 COMPETITION WINNERS

Relinquenda by Alexandra Lytton Regalado
Chosen by Reginald Betts for Beacon Press

Symmetry of Fish by Su Cho
Chosen by Paige Lewis for Penguin Books

Harbinger by Shelley Puhak
Chosen by Nicole Sealey for Ecco

Extinction Theory by Kien Lam
Chosen by Kyle Dargan for University of Georgia Press

Ask the Brindled_Indigiqueer Poetry from Hawai'i by No'u Revilla
Chosen by Rick Barot for Milkweed Editions

RELINQUENDA

Alexandra Lytton Regalado

BEACON PRESS · BOSTON

BEACON PRESS
Boston, Massachusetts
www.beacon.org

Beacon Press books
are published under the auspices of
the Unitarian Universalist Association of Congregations.

25 24 23 22   8 7 6 5 4 3 2 1

This book is printed on acid-free paper that meets the uncoated
paper ANSI/NISO specifications for permanence as revised in 1992.

Text design and composition by Michael Starkman
at Wilsted & Taylor Publishing Services.

The poem "Crush," by Andrés Montoya, is used
here by permission of the Estate of Andrés Montoya.

LIBRARY OF CONGRESS CATALOGING-IN-PUBLICATION DATA

Names: Regalado, Alexandra Lytton, author.
Title: Relinquenda / Alexandra Lytton Regalado.
Description: Boston : Beacon Press, [2022] | This work is one of five 2021
    National Poetry Series competition winners. | Summary: "The poems of
    Relinquenda (Latin: relinquish) take place between Miami, Florida, and El
    Salvador, and they center on themes of impermanence and the body,
    communication and inarticulation, and the broken and mended ties of
    family relationships"— Provided by publisher.
Identifiers: LCCN 2022013000 | ISBN 9780807007105 (trade paperback ;
    acid-free paper) | ISBN 9780807007112 (ebook)
Subjects: LCGFT: Poetry.
Classification: LCC PS3618.E446 R44 2022 | DDC 811/.6—dc23
    /eng/20220317
LC record available at https://lccn.loc.gov/2022013000

In memory of my father.

&

For Tomás.

Nadie en jade,
nadie en oro se convertirá:
En la tierra quedará guardado.
Todos nos iremos
allá, de igual modo.
—NEZAHUALCÓYOTL

Renunciation – is a piercing Virtue –
The letting go
A Presence
—EMILY DICKINSON

relinquendus

Latin

Participle

relinquendus m (*feminine* **relinquenda**, *neuter* **relinquendum**); *first/second declension*

    1. which is to be <u>abandoned</u>, which is to be <u>relinquished</u>

CONTENTS

RELINQUENDA

Relinquenda

The snake always slips into the bushes when I start down the path.
The snake is just the tail end of what's happening.
The snake doesn't look back.
The snake is not an animal I identify with.
I mean, it's a garden-variety queen snake but I'd still lop off its head with a machete.
Isn't it expected that one thing will chase another?
Isn't it normal to want your space?

About this snake, it's not the kind that holds its tail in its mouth.
About this machete, I do not own one.
About this path, I chose it.
It's narrow.

About this metaphor, it stretches out like a tightrope.
And these lines force one foot in front of the other.
And these steps are the ones I have to take.

About the snake, I must circle back.

About the time I left the door open.
About the zero surprise I felt when our eyes locked.

As if what I needed was a mirror.
As though I would always lead her in & back her into a corner.

As soon as I extend my hands, she coils into her self.
As soon as I take another step, she slashes the cord.

I.

Mamá Tacuazín

It's the middle of the night & there's the creaking heft of a creature,
the scabbering of nails in the crawlspace above our bedroom.

We'd fallen asleep angry, you'd raised your voice, cursed
in front of our daughter & slammed the door. I'd felt in the pit

of my stomach a clawed animal digging in. All these nights I lay
sleepless while you snored at my side. But this is no dream, this thing

scrambling above us & now, I'm wide awake gauging the animal's weight
& wondering if the ceiling is enough to contain it. Was this the possum

that weeks ago knocked over my orchid pots, hid in the palms & ate
their red rosary of seeds, that finally the gardener caught by the scruff

of its neck? I'd begged them not to kill it, instead to set it free
at the corner park & let it live where nothing would chase it. But there,

in the grip of a gloved hand, the animal's pebble eyes were flat black,
its long snout hanging slack & lined with sharp teeth & I thought it

dead already but when I stepped closer, pinned to its white underbelly
were six squirming pink babies who'd not yet learned to play dead.

Now, above our bedroom, nails clatter & I imagine the possum ripping
out wires, clawing up plaster. How was it the possum returned

to our yard, managed to escape our husky who'd recently torn apart
our daughter's pet rabbit, to scamper up the palm trees & across

the one frond arcing over the roof & find the broken clay tile
that leads to the crawlspace above our heads? To stay inert was also

a choice & an action. When my mother got married, my great-aunt
gave her one piece of advice, which was passed down to me: A veces

hay que hacerse la inútil. Don't be so quick to resolve everything. No seás
tan arrecha or you'll never get a break. My husband sits up in bed

& asks what's that noise? I wish for that possum mother to dig in,
to make a den in that house we've just sold. Her enterprise disturbs you,

husband. You call out my name & I stay silent.

Hija, an Inheritance

Of pink, I relate only to red's
Snakebite strike, to white's muffled

Light, the two like foods on a child's plate,
Colors that must remain untouching.

Pink rabbit eye, pretty yet sinister;
The signs along the trafficked road

To the beach offer *Rabbits: For Meat
Or Pets*. When I was a child, our pet rabbit

Lived in a cage in the far corner of our yard
& beyond that fence lay acres & acres

Of government land set aside for experiments
On fruit trees. Pink like that dwarf-rabbit's

Gums, I obsessed with her teeth & I'd
Turn the rabbit on her back, cup her in the palm

Of my hand & part her furred lips. She did not mean
To smile & it was funny. She always bit me, but it

Was worth it. Pink as a young girl's bedroom, the heart
Of a seashell, our own pink interior, the meat of us, pink

Of lip: red, what it says yes to; white, what is unsaid.
Pink inside of rabbit ears, always

At attention, I'd pet the softest parts &
They'd turn, following their fear.

The Giantess

After Leonora Carrington's painting
After Tracy K. Smith

Daughter, you need to grow into your body,
understand its dimensions,
how to move in this world.
I tell her this as she mops up water
from a glass she's knocked over.
She is constantly bumping, tripping,
leaving frames askew.
She hides in hoodies & sweats,
but the girl is all legs, taller than me
at thirteen. I want her live in her body,
not padded in layers of fabric, shoulders
hunched, veiled in long hair, behind
glasses. Push it back, I tell her,
I want to see your pretty face,
in the voice of all women, telling all
other women how to be seen.
She talks of feminism, tells her brothers
Mami will disown you if you are not
a feminist; quick to bark, quick to snap,
to claw, to sink in a tooth.
            Arrows & daggers at her feet
& her moon head overcast, as she watches
wide-winged geese circle her body. A family
takes refuge between her ankles,
us or her future family. A lumen cape
hangs from her shoulders, but the egg—
all sun—she holds close to her chest.
How to be a tower, a pillar
of confidence, to inhabit that body
at thirteen, still surprised to be on this earth—
how is it that things work? Do you want to play
a game with me? She wants to skate on smooth

streets, go out into the world without someone
shadowing her. She wants to live in her skin.
I bite back my anger at her awkwardness,
show tenderness for the fawn stumbling
to find its legs, mewling kitten. She is far from
these helpless animals. Wolf at the foot
of her bed, she draws or reads, curtains shut
in a freezing room. She doesn't belong to me
as much as her body belongs to her.
I look up to her, rising stories
above me, rising above her own body
&—haven't I seen her
elsewhere & before—she
is what waits to be said.

Videofeed from the American Embassy of El Salvador

Ferns grow in the storm gutter / mamá
admires their hard work / fronds curl
between the grates / when the sewer
overbrims in rain / her eyes never /
mamá holds back / lines of people lean
against the fence / for the stamp that will
open the gate / she knows what feeds the
ferns / survive & survive not much else /
when her child stumbles, falls / look the
other way / the wound, the fingers / in
the wound / the wounds glimmering &
mumbling their blood / she must shift
the child's attention / don't cry, keep
going // stay there don't pan out

                    mamá will crumple like a brown leaf & other
                    women / will hold her up / she wants to eat
                    handfuls of dirt / the dirt that soaked up her child's
                    blood / no mourning garb but a diadem of grey
                    hairs // stay there don't pan out // the newspaper
                    roses with names of the dead / one for thirst one
                    for hunger seamless desert & sky / mamá's sadness
                    doesn't break shore or evaporate into cloud / hands
                    she rubs together like dried twigs // camera eye /
                    don't flinch keep your gaze

I Prided Myself on Being Aguantadora

As a verb "shoring up" // not the verb "keening" as in to cry
Entre más doy, más tengo // entre más agua entrego, más se llena la fuente
Tengo sed, drink the vinegar // prayer is a call & response, dear sister,
Press the wafer to your tongue, tilt the cup // or pass a thorny rope
Through your tongue, // there will be a scroll of blood to burn.
Al exhalar, I hear
My name. Breathe the pain // to get to something good—How
Do we learn that? Birth, yes, birth, // or our mouths clenched
On a rope of muscle. When moved to ecstasy // or despair our mouths only know
How to make round sounds, our lips // puckered & twisted into ovals, ellipses
And all forms of circles, a howl knows to empty // a body, a cenote, a cave,
Dear sister, all things dark & carved out, water hollowing // over a course
Of decades landmasses made in duress. In this, my role is // seawall, resist
And resist & let it come.
Al extender, I hear my name. I hear
Often: "He llorado lo que no está escrito," & I hold // my shoulder firm
Against the surge. A hammer // to a finger reveals our mother // tongue; we say
Ow // or ay & silently we count with our lips // in our language cut
With the deepest grooves. Pain as something we need to cross, // a threshold
We move through // as it is sometimes a car peeling out of a driveway,
White pebbles // striking bare shins, one sharp rock, dear sister,
How it could also be a pebble in a shoe. Click of stone // on stone,
Sting of stone on skin, I skidded along // that edge: daughter mother woman;
I was a stone set against pain & she threw // herself at my feet.

El Puente Que Nos Une

I left red gladiolas on the altar.

      Patrón Santiago Apostól, your horse is spattered with mud.

San Alejo, your shoes are worn.

      Acompáñanos y líbranos de todo mal.

This bridge is long and rickety.

      Rotten planks, rusted nails moan every step.

Who built this?

      We've had to leap across all that collapsed.

I have no choice.

      Can't stop to ask why.

Can't rest.

      There are people in front of us and people behind us.

The way back would be just as long.

      Best to keep going.

We must get to the other side.

      Con cada paso mi sombra pierde color.

The dark water offers my face and I say to it:

      This is my one and only life.

Already others are pressing up behind me.

      And others have moved too far ahead.

When someone falls I cannot stop to help.

      Even though some look like Papá, but younger.

Mamá, but mixed with my daughter's face.

      An old friend who died long ago.

Patrón, who will save us?

      Will I turn into a fish if I fall?

Will I be jolted awake?

A Family History of Alcoholism

With my father it's all about waiting.
I fling the baited hook into the canal, beyond the limestone's yellow o's
of fossilized shells—how easily it crumbles!
The plastic slats of the aluminum chair brand my thighs.
My father pops a beer beneath his white bucket hat, smokes his cigarette
down to the nub & with a flick sends it skipping.
I toss bits of squashed white loaf at the wart-faced ducks
that huff in the shallows; I poke through a gauze of mosquito eggs
& watch two-legged tadpoles map the shoreline.
But then my line bobs, my rod buckles, my chair skittering
across the rocky ledge. I lunge for the rod,
struggle to right myself on the slope, my feet mucked in algae,
the rod whips & I turn to my dad, his mouth pulled
into a tight line—keep your footing—he grits.
I snap the rod back, quick sizzle of the reel & when I haul up
that long grey fish—my first—it cuts the air with its pointed rayfins,
its silver dollar eye & grinning jaws. I know, from here on out,
this beast I lured & wrangled to shore, the fight is mine alone.

Cavities Are Inherited

After the song "Sad Eyes," Robert John, 1979

Dr. Mahaffey warns us to take it easy on the sweet tooth,
tells my mom our cavities are inherited. Sad music
pipes through the dentist office speakers, old people singing

about broken hearts & things I don't understand. Why do people
only sing about love, I ask my mom on a trip to Sears
where the pigeons roost on the belly of the S. Where once I saw

a bird hanging from its neck on a wire. Now they put spikes on signs
to keep the birds from making nests. While our mother shops,
my sisters & I play hide & seek in the clothes racks

& she pretends we are not her children. If we drop something
she warns us behind clenched teeth & secretly pinches our arms.
At the bank I look through her purse; my mother carries so much.

I tear slips of paper & make drawings of mice climbing ladders
of bisected dollhouses. For me, once Barbie's house is set up
there is nothing else to play. I don't know their dramas.

My drama is only the kitten *Hang In There* poster in Dr. Mahaffey's office.
The treasure chest of Five & Dime stuff little kids are tricked into.
But I am beyond those ploys. We were being anesthetized,

warned of all that's sweet. Then, that time I saw Dr. Mahaffey
& I thought—Bruce—the whole other side of him, in a red convertible,
top down, feathered 70s hair in the late 80s, in shiny cop glasses,

driving alongside our stationwagon. I watched him tilt back the dregs
of a can of Budweiser, cranking music, some American band
that peaked too soon or that never peaked at all. Remembering

his bare hands in my mouth, fingers smelling of apple cinnamon soap,
& singing into my face, *Sad eyes, you knew there'd come a day,*
as he drilled & my mouth opening wider, as wide as it could go.

Elegy with Wisdom Teeth

For two nights she'd left it under her pillow & I'd forgotten
to leave the customary note & five-dollar bill.
They're falling out too frequently.

She returns from school with her prize rattling
in a tooth-shaped locket around her neck.
Her body breaking off all remnants
of its baby shell. She wakes with aching shins,
yowling in pain. Sure, there's the warbling song
of lullabies, snapshots of sleeping babies, but no way
to record the memory of touch—kisses, caresses,
the waning moon of a fever sweat.

I told my children there was no Tooth Fairy, that it's Ratón Pérez
who collects teeth for his mouse wife. She likes
to fashion molars & cuspids into tiaras, pendants
& rings. How vain of her to want so much
jewelry, my daughter says.

One Halloween I dressed as the Tooth Fairy,
wore my wisdom teeth as dangly earrings.
They'd been surgically removed & for years
I'd kept them in a box beneath the sink.
The tentacle-length of the roots astonishing
& I thought them beautiful & mysterious, why
I wrapped the molars in wire & secured them
with pliers into hook posts.

But at the party no one thought my earrings funny;
they were flat-out disgusted, as if I were parading around
some kind of bad taxidermy, a human bone
pierced through my septum, a cannibal's prize.
No tusk, no claw to confer power or spirit,
what's left over, what—once it leaves
our body—is alien, fingernail clippings,

a piece of skin on the mat of a karate dojo,
an old Band-Aid, a soaked maxi pad, all
that is wiped & flushed, reviled.

I sense the shipwreck, my human body
sloughed off, cast away, sunbleached
& bonewhite driftwood on a beach
where my children will gather around
the wreckage as it singes & cracks,
into wind, ashes, everything I returned to,
clung to, there & there & there,
painting their faces, their empty hands,
there, there.

How to Crack an Egg

I am not a woman who has a way with fruit;
my hands cannot divine through touch when flesh
is ready for the knife. That small window
when sweetness peaks & everything is willing.

What I know of my father is still green,
will likely never ripen. My own heart still
wrapped in letters from years ago, the ones he wrote
with his perfect hands, long fingers & clipped nails.

Such is his work ethic: simple, honest. We can aspire to smell of soap,
like bricklayers leaving a construction site, wet hair slicked back,
wearing a shirt sunned on a tree branch all the workday,
for the two-hour bus ride to the family & a plate of hot food.

My father needs precision—engineer's eyes,
carpenter's hands, everything plumb & square.
He seeks symmetry & durability,
things that last & question obsolescence.

His own father, my grandfather, builder of bridges,
El Puente de Oro razed during the war,
now only an oxidized pillar above the muddy banks
of the Río Lempa, river the color of a brown egg.

On the couch, Saturday cartoons on the TV,
my father's fingertips curved together
to form an invisible egg he'd crack on my kneecap
& his fingers dripped the yolk.

My father was happy when he fed us;
he'd set the plate before me
& I'd bite my cuticles, pick at the ragged edge,
till I tasted the rusted iron of my blood.

That fried egg on a plate, what he handed over,
those weekends, fingertips on my knee,
that soft tapping to be let in,
cracked open & poured out.

Hands Just Like Two Balloons

 After a writing conference on the coast of Oregon, two new friends offer me a ride back to the city. Julie, a taxi driver & poet, says the mountain pass will cut a half hour of driving time. In the backseat, Abigail, twenty years younger than both of us, chats in an awkward-genius fashion about the role of ants in surreal art. I'm all too familiar with her style of unfiltered honesty, the pebble-drop ease of shutting down & the silence that ripples around her. On my nighttable back home the books referencing the autistic spectrum were wrapped in cloth covers because I didn't want my kids wondering which of them I was investigating. I'd been grinding my teeth, breaking molars even with a night guard, & my husband had assured me that I needed a break, that my manuscript locked in a drawer during a decade of motherhood had to be unearthed, no reason to feel guilty, no matter that it was the kids' first week back to school after Christmas break. One hour into the drive the road becomes steeper & I lean into the windshield to video the forest of snowcapped pines on the winding road. For them this wintry scene is as postcard clichéd as my Salvadoran miles of black sand beaches. We don't hear the weather warning because Julie is playing a Pink Floyd box set. The first snowflakes come at us like tumbling moths. It's for my kids, I say as I film. As we drive further the trees crowd the road, pressing their snowy shoulders together. A half hour later, cars start pulling over, people stand ankle-deep in snow to put chains on their tires. I wonder if we should be worried. But Julie drives on, chatting with Abigail about Robert Frost & the suicidal bullshit people read into his poems. The sky is totally blotted out & the wipers smear across a soupy landscape. My phone rings & I'm surprised there's service in this pocket, surprised to hear my son's voice on the line. His Sunday afternoon voice, dreading school, dreading the hours of look-me-in-the-eye, the hours of get-your head-out-of-the-clouds. My husband switches on, apologizes for having tapped out of patience—is this a bad time? Julie & Abigail are silent & David Gilmour's crooning doesn't seem loud enough. Then my son on the line again & his warbled pleas. I switch to Spanish, cool & collected, I make my words sit up straight, my tone of voice takes the guise of a caress, something like the way I touch his hair. They would think me coddling, overprotective. He has trouble with transitions, I cover the mouthpiece to explain. The snow goes on, smothering everything. Keep it even & reassuring: I understand, I understand; listen & then distract. The car grows hot; I need to kick off the featherdown, open a window. More snow, the slow snake of cars & bleary red eyes of brake lights. There is no visible end to this mountain pass.

Hacer de Tripas Corazón

With lines by Rainer Maria Rilke and Joy Harjo

For beauty is nothing
      but the beginning of terror,
is what you must've thought
      when you arrived at the high desert.
Sleeping alone beneath a tarp,
      your breath cut with cactus blooms & thistle.
The counselors showed you how to saw branches
      of juniper & sagebrush to build your pack,
how to whittle a spoon & spindle for fire-making,
      to trek the miles of eleven weeks.
Often a star was waiting / For you to notice it.
      At home the bluebottle flies still trapped
in your bedroom, highest corner of our house.
      The flies pitch headfirst into glass,
urging me out of sleep.
      As a child you'd appear at our bedside asking
please kill the fly humming & buzzing me awake.
      You'd once seen a fly birthing maggots
on your bedspread; nightmares for years.
      We'd snap the hand towel at the ceiling
until the fly landed stunned,
      dead on the tiles, then flush it down the toilet
& everyone back to bed. Now, years later,
      a wind full of infinite space gnawing at our faces.
You, in the high desert,
      where wilderness not only means survival,
but "adventure therapy, resilience for troubled teens"—
      we did the right thing, the counselors say,
hay que hacer de tripas corazón, los abuelos say,
      while I try to fashion a heart from my tangle of guts—
you spend afternoons catching flies between your palms;
      the flies fat & lazy from heat,
even they must submit
      & you pinch off their wings & they are reduced

to ground insects, your pets.

       Stubbing flies, you wrote in your letters,
the way I'd seen my father put out a cigarette,

       orange ember pressed to glass until it gives
& folds in on itself. The fire you, my son, struggled

       to make—I closed my eyes & saw your hands rubbing
the spindle back & forth, twisting it into the groove

       of the board, the toprock tight in your hand,
again & again you faltered & it fell apart.

       For any spark to make a song
it must be transformed under pressure.

       De tripas corazón, you kept trying & weeks later—
unspeakable need, muscle of belief—

       the rubbing of your hands produced coal;
you learned to make a nest of juniper bark,

       small hairs concentrated in the center,
you placed the coal in the heart of the nest,

       brought it close to your lips & blew, waving
the flames alive, the snap of green wood resisting.

Caracol

It'll be fast

the nurse told me as he stroked my head / not the side encrusted with glass but the bloodless side where my hair was dry not matted & sticky / & said to me like a father he said sorry I'm sorry / but I have to tell you / ruptured spleen, shattered pelvis, internal bleeding the doctors said / I want to tell you the nurse said they are going to drill into your bone / there's nothing more to dull the pain my stomach filled with blood & swollen / this is going to hurt the nurse said / there is no other way to say this but

It'll be fast

Is no consolation

When there is a body   Moving over you

And you are there & not   There   Not there not there

Hands moving over you

Whether it's hands   Metal instruments

Or faith   To cave inside you   Tell your self   Let your self

Let   Let   Let

Seawall & the swell

Tumble

To seaglass

A child my child running on a beach look mamá / look mamá what I found perfect a shell & he uncurls his fingers / tiny nailbeds perfect scallops translucent & the whorled & glistening pink / of his palm gripping a broken caracol I'd tossed aside because— spiral staircase, exposed ribcage—it was broken / & he with his tiny white teeth / insists I take it & I take it because it is now because of him, perfect

It'll be

Fast   It'll be   fast

Tires skidding   explosion of glass

Metal accordioned   My body thrown   A tree felled

Strip   The pain   Shaft to root   Pulled clean

Soil in nailbeds

Bloody from scratching

Mamá always said spit & make a cross   On a bite

Itch   And deny the urge

Hollow the shell   The voice that echoes & echoes

You hold it to your ear & hear the cry   The heartbeat   Pounding

The seawall   The swell

                    The seaglass perfect
      Because it is broken   And without   Edges dulled to
          A prize   The pain   I held it gripped in my palm
                        It'll be fast
                  Is not what the doctor said

as he stroked my hair the unmatted & unbloodied side the one not embedded / with glass
shards from the shattered car window / know this / will be the worst pain / more than
any pain more than / the child you will one day carry & birth / my shattered pelvis then
an unsolvable / puzzle a broken basket a collapsed labyrinth / antiseptic white the light
& the doctors wiping / my body down hands moving over me / the nurse stroked my
face & looked me in the eyes & said / ready & they held my arms down they held me /
& the drill revved & they held me & the drill / channeled deep its cry into bone

II.

What My Father Taught Me About Black Holes

The ghost of my father haunts me
      While he is still alive.
Thank you, he tells me, but
      I don't like poetry.
His body beneath the sheet
      Spotlit through gap-tooth
Shutters. On the bedskirt yellow
      Arcs, wheels of urine,
Marks to say do not go
      There. Not like the cat that rubs
Its face to say this is mine.
      Our tiny white dog, foxlike, but old &
Toothless just a stinking gap
      Of a mouth, lifts his leg daily
So we have to lock the room
      Where my father sleeps.
My father or a pillow beneath
      That white sheet. The rays of light
Enter. They have to rest
      Somewhere. When my father says
Goodbye, he says instead, take it
      Easy. He eases into the bed,
Takes it, the light falling where it wants.

Probably the Most My Father Has Ever Said to Me

Little plants grew out of my feet. Not vines, not branches
with leaves, no, it was clover, bright green. It's the last
thing I remember when the phone rang at 3am,
I picked up, no one was there. In the morning,
still wondering, I walked to the sideyard; the wind
had knocked down the climbing bougainvillea,
yanked down part of the fence; it was all brambles
& thorns & the thick trunk had split, broken
the ceramic pot, ripped its roots from the asphalt.
I'm not sure it can be saved.   Each year
your mother lugs the heavy clippers & prunes it back,
gives it shape, always finishes the day with scratches
up her forearms—but she likes to do it; it gives her
pleasure like the way she hoses down the entrance
& sends leaves & berries down little eddies
& into a puddle at the foot of the driveway.
I stood in front of the broken bougainvillea
& looked up at the zigzag of telephone wires
where there was a little brown dove coo-cooing
& I was amazed—the bird turned his head left
& right as it watched two buzzards gliding high
on a thermal & I thought, surely, that brown bird
was looking out for traffic the way a child is taught
to look both ways before crossing a street—
but now on second thought I bet that bird was thinking:
I wish I could do that.

The Hero Myth

1.

Veni Vidi Vici, Julius Caesar's words on the Marlboro pack
sold a feeling: a swift & conclusive victory.
Plato postulated: a visual fire burns
between our eyes & that which they behold.
Between bucking horses & a gold crown
this man rides hard for a living.
What kind of man are you? Can you do the cowboy's trick:
high in the saddle, gripping reins, the one-handed shake of box,
pluck the cigarette between your lips
& spark the lighter?
He is his own man
& a cigarette is good company.

2.

The spider's web is a home & a trap.
My mourning is meshed.
I cry for other men because I can't cry for my father.
A leak that can't find an escape
pools to the other extreme.
The heart is circuitous.
The dentist says I am suffering from *desgaste*;
am I grinding stones, or learning to polish,
my molars snap into silence.
Father, you are Houdini, you slipped
from the chains & disappeared without saying goodbye.
Don Eddie, you were also Don('t) Falldown, Don('t) Do That—
What your mother called out as she followed you,
a toddler going up the stairs (worry is useful,
possibly lifesaving) & in others' ears
twisted into titles to honor the forbidden.

3.

All signs point to a black hole.
Even light cannot escape it &
you should resist, but you lead on
against the waves. You need proof,
the world's cameras clicking at once,
& it is there, a monster's eye, luring us
to those places forbidden; swim with mask & fins
into the cave, to see what was never meant to be seen
by human eyes. Science answered for you,
but what does your heart say, Father?
Sos necio, terco, leaning into the pit.
A tunnel, the tip of your cigarette,
bottom of the bottle drawing you in.
Will you tell me on that final day
how you stared into that eye this entire time?

4.

The myopic eye cannot see what is directly before it.
About the things of the world & the mind
looking at the things of the world,
let it sing through me.
Say it harsh, say the truth.
Take off the thorny crown;
the thirst for drink is in our genes
& how I ducked that bullet is an oil painting,
mother & child with hands posed in praise,
eyes rolling in ecstasy, of the moment seized
& rendered purely. The poet says it all
& my father who says nothing
is stone, is statue. He laid all the groundwork.
The break is still there, but healing.
The gold poured into the fracture,
let it sing through me.

5.

"El que por su gusto muere,
que lo entierren parado."
Let it sing through me,
search the grass for kindling;
how I was taught to kneel on a stick
& break it. The popping of green firewood,
hard to light, hard to burn,
we smolder in the fires
of previous skins.

Drownproofing

In the pool something floats on the surface,
                            & you pray please God
let it be a leaf but that bulk is something dead,
                            a winged thing spiraling
in a wind eddy in the deep end, a mourning dove,
                            & you already hip-deep in the shallow end.
You break a hydrangea leaf to shroud its body,
                            the curved pink claws clasp nothing but air.
Across the lawn still the swallows
                            dive to pluck insects mid-flight.
And you will not fling that bird's body
                            over the wall, but rather place it on the box-hedge,
& you will watch as if through a pane of glass
                            how the sun presses down on the dove's body,
its blue-rimmed eye aimed at the clouds.
                            You will stand hip-deep in the wind-ruffled pool,
knowing there were wings there.
                            You float, turning in the eddies,
your wings stretched out, trying not to sink.

Invasive

They nest in the poinciana tree outside my childhood bedroom;
the peacocks call out their strange noise before dawn: a child's wail,
a woman's shriek, a strangled cat. My father coughs, a laugh, a cry,

an alarm he is still flesh & blood. We are here to wait it out.
All day, in the leather recliner, my father watches cooking programs
& game shows. Death is wild, we are told. He is both hunter & prey,

a stooped grey bird & a gape-mouthed fish in a tank rounding
out vowels through the glass: Gone, Gone. Iguanas slink through the grass,
a greener green in the backyard, & they chew on fallen avocados.

Each visit my father is frailer, less of him, thin as a letter I once wrote
& never mailed, *Dear Motherest & Fatherleast*, will never mail.
Now I spend nights watching period-piece movies with my mother

& days cooking food my father will turn away. Outside, these Florida non-native
species: peafowl, iguana & python learn to navigate our human lives,
lurking in backyards, roosting in trees, eating seeds unsuited for them.

Where is home or origin? Not wanting to be consoled for such a loss,
that should be our instinct. Iguanas prowl the porch & rip the screens
with their talons, wag the red flags of their wrinkled chins.

I wait, not for them, but for the peacock family that visits every afternoon.
The brown peachick turns his clock eye to my palm-full of seeds.
The neighbors annoyed that I've lured the peacocks, by the human-sized

shits on their driveways. A nuisance, they say, we'll sic our dog on them.
Too real, their foul & loud beauty. And all I want is for the peacocks
to eat from my palm. If it were that easy to find the right words, to hand them

over, watch them be swallowed & hear the cluck of happiness.
My father reads detective novels with his sweating glass
& nest of cigarette butts stubbed so hard into the edges of the ashtray,

the shapes fold over as if begging for forgiveness. He pees in the backyard
& we pretend not to notice, let him do what he wants. He is eternal
as the native palmetto bug. We fear how it pauses knowingly

before it skitters in wild directions, flying towards us or flattening
into any crevice. Wings of butterfly, wings of roach, who would mourn
their absence? My sister traps iguanas in the backyard; they eat

the tender shoots, entire flowerbeds of impatiens. Their spiny bodies
whiptail over the paving stones, sun their bellies all morning long.
In the Everglades, it's open season year-round for pythons. Abandoned pets,

hand-fed pink mice & warm beneath a bulb, now wild & mating,
birthing up to a hundred hatchlings no one wants. But a fanged creature,
backed into a corner, poisonous or not, will lash out. We need

to let them be, my mother says. A dying person needs a moment alone;
he can't let go when you're holding his hand. I imagine reading Rumi
to my father because his ears will be the last to go, the window open

& a breeze lifting the curtain, outside the moon in its feathered crown.
But I also know I could step out for just one moment, to pee,
or to see if the clouds have parted their skirts & that is when

he will die. In that moment, when the others are asleep, & in that space
between breaths, he will take to the air in a wing-flap, slink beneath
the dark surface of that unknown world without even a ripple.

Vesper Bells

It's raining now, unexpected in this month, & the rain could be an audience clapping,
      could be fire splitting logs. Hearts red as the geraniums
nodding yes & yes & the rains' downpour on pavement has finally silenced the sound of
      the oxygen machine
in the next room as it clangs through its cycle, a wave rising & washing over the room
      with each breath, the extinguishing shush closing
with a distant churchbell's toll. Only I hear it, how it urges me to stand before the altar,
      asking: Have you answered this call?
The rain lulls & I wish it would storm, something to flush this cotton-bound drift though
      days. A poet said—was it Rilke?—
presence is prayer, presence is love. And so we should haul ourselves up, put our pens
      down, look into our beloved's eyes & dare.
I'm ready to put that into letters, papers to be read later, but not uttered aloud, even if it
      is my own blood, my father, or my child.
My firstborn son would look at me from his crib with eyes like lamps, a tower of light
      searching. I was the dark rocks.
How to live in that light? How could I hold it without also warning of all I could wreck?
      Even then, I knew that light would wane, as it happens
in all of us. I get older & realize I've never been able to be silly; how I resist the
      spotlight. If I dance it'll be in the corner of a dark room
where the speaker booms through my body the way the geraniums sway in wind. But the
      rain outside has also hesitated & the bell
of the oxygen machine calls out its clocked alarm, a barb, a notch, a gavel. I try to tune it
      out but things swim to the surface; the moment is there
& there again, has been there for six years now, my father dying in the next room & still
      I have not found a way to lean
into his ear & say what I need to say. There is my son again, swimming up in memory,
      how he looked up at me wanting me to lean
down & whisper into his ear, words he didn't even understand yet—but it was in the
      leaning in that I would speak.
I felt terrified & looked away. I am ashamed now to say this, remembering how I also
      felt pins in the soles of my feet
when, at fifteen, I stood atop a bridge railing & leaped into a canal at night, to swim
      through the brown water over the silt
littered with rusted & sharp discards, & how I laughed as I reached the shore where my
      friends waited, also laughing.

How to lean into this distance? Would it be enough to fill in all those blanks, those
things unsaid, perhaps even, unfelt? That was the terror—
how my father would respond. It is clockwork, this moment, & it is expected I give my
solemn & sincere goodbye. I am his child
& I need to forgive him for all those years our lights never merged. The rain wavers, the
plants are still, the world is slick
with meaning. I think of leaning into my child's crib, how we could easily transpose our
bodies like the hands of a clock, tick forward.
My father's eyes are closed; he has not spoken or taken food or drink for three days. I
could be speaking into my own cupped hand.
The rain picks up, I anticipate the whoosh of air, the breath, the wave, my own heart's
clanging & lean in. It rains & the pavement breaks into diamonds.

What My Father Taught Me About Evolution

Claws have little ambiguity, this I have come to understand.
And this Thanksgiving our family is the portrait of a grotesque,
the auctioned painting no one bids for. It does not match the living room
couch. There is no aesthetic consideration in death. Wild & free,
there's no taming it. Will come as it pleases, there's no coaxing.
No tiptoe through the grass to eat out of the palm of my hand.
These are my father's last sounds: is it a cry, a laugh, a cough
so hard to tell if he's breathing. His hundred-pound self curled into a shell,
no, more hermit crab without a shell. But there's nothing soft:
he is all angles, all knees & elbows. His face cut into the death mask,
the skull plain & visible, his eyes sunken & when I put my hands
around him, to wrap his blanket tighter I squeeze his foot to say
all set, he cries out loudly. I remove his sock & his toenails
are so long they curl under his toes. Like our childhood dog,
a Lassie, that hobbled on overgrown nails & the vet said
he could have pressed charges against us for neglect.
And it was twenty some years ago I witnessed our dog's death.
How he searched for a corner, crawled beneath a table,
wanted to escape through any open door but I kept pulling him
to me, to stay, to hold him up so he could breathe,
my twenty-year-old self still imagining I could save others.
There is no metaphor here, it was in effect, a death
& the dog went in the most horrible moaning like Chewbacca,
banging his head against the table legs, his limbs shaking,
his body rattling in a pool of piss, shit & blood, snapped off
the tip of his own tongue. It would have been humane
to put him down. But we thought it better to let nature run its course,
he was old, we thought, let it happen the way it was intended.
But there was nothing natural in wrapping our twelve-year-old dog
in a beach towel & setting his body in the back of my car
to drop it off in the rain, to be cremated, while the rest of the family
was at my brother's high school graduation. It was my first death
& now my father is calling out that he's cold, that he wants a drink,
that he needs to get up to smoke. That night I cut off the thick, yellow
crescents of his nails, afraid I'd cut into his skin, & placed them
in a pile on the nightstand, a shell midden, & for a second

I thought about keeping them, how my artist friend had done,
kept his cut nails in an urn for an entire year, a memento of his mortality.
My father in his hospital bed, the final step before the coffin, all the things
he's had to submit to at the slippery slope above the grave.
My artist friend formed words out of his nail crescents—AMOR—
& glazed them onto a canvas. That is the art no one wants hanging
in their living room, a mirror to remind us how our own nails
continue to grow in the coffin. Claws are unambiguous,
to attack, to defend, proof we were here on this earth living
among other beings. Tonight, we share food at Thanksgiving,
we set the table with wreaths, with apples, candles & flowers
& poems about the harvest moon & cook our grandmother's recipes,
the pies he might like to eat, what he has already let go of, food only
a memory now. This is enough, the night nurse tells me, the smell
is what fills him. Thanksgiving was my father's holiday. He showed us
love in the most traditional sense, putting food on the table.
He'd see us eating & enjoying it & feel satisfied by the work
of his hands. His hands are what I hold, strong grip,
smooth skin, these are the hands I have inherited,
though I worry at them, bite my cuticles to the quick.
This is what he has passed on, written with amor,
on a blank canvas & gilt frame. There,
next to his death bed as he claws for his next breath.

Escape Room

1.

The lineup of snubbed-out butts in
the empty cigarette box, hard evidence
of how many per day & not what he tells the doctors.
Beer bottles tossed in the trash bin;
I've lost count.

2.

"Such a constitution," say the doctors. "You've done everything
you can to kill your body & still it won't quit!" But
he's afraid of the needle. It has to be something
so thin & sharp to get into that thick skin.
This man who travelled with a gun under the driver's
seat. The zippered bag I remember seeing
in his nightstand, feeling the burnished leather
with a single finger. Does one hand know
what the other hand does?

3.

He tells a story: "When I was a boy, my friend & I used to go down to the Mississippi
River. We spent all day digging in the muddy bank with the idea of building a cave, our
clubhouse. The plan was to sleep there, but my friend chickened out in the end & I
followed him home. The next day the whole thing had collapsed. Luck or fear kept us
alive."

4.

He rubs his hands on his knees as if he's warming himself up before a long walk.
He wanted to play classical guitar, listened to Gitano music & Don McLean's
      "American Pie"—that song
crying out its chorus about the devil & the end of the American Dream.
The dead musicians flew to North Dakota in bad weather, the song 8½ minutes long,
      a hit in 1972, the year I was born,
my father's first, a daughter. "There is no poetry & very little romance in anything
      anymore," said McLean.

5.

Moon clouded over, I play my father's song
on the drive home. He's fallen for the third time
in one month, syncope, cut his forehead & broken
his arm & somehow managed to drag himself
to bed, a soldier to the trench, too drunk to feel pain
until he wakes up the next morning & calls
out to us saying his body is useless.

6.

He's   unraveling   while I'm still   knitting us,   the cloth pulled &
    snagged,   letting in   light. I undo   my mistakes,   trace
    back to the first stitch.

7.

When we speak of you
in the third person, you are
in the room the way a stone
marks an absence.

8.

As I pass through the hall, my father
is the one I see in every doorway, sitting
on the edge of the bed, & when I return
to check, he's gone, like a haze
of insects, more air than body.

9.

He tells another story: "When I was a boy I used to climb the giant elm in our front yard.
Near the top, a branch broke & I fell till I was about one foot above the ground. I hung
there in disbelief, suspended by the belt loop of my Levi's that had caught on a snapped
branch."

10.

My mother says he has to be in the ground
for these poems to be born.

The tree in our front yard
I machete
to its milk heart.

Turning the Stone, Contrapuntal

After Andrés Montoya

Their translucent bodies stitch the white sheet,	*surely*
trace a seam in his arm hairs, a vein of marching bodies	*the ants came*
to the oracular circle, ghostprint	*from their hills*
of a sweating beer bottle on the nightstand,	*of crushed fruit*
their tiny bodies cast into tar pits, cherry	*they crawled poemlike—*
pools of spit-up cough drops.	*o, how I wish for the sea*
Tracing paths made by scent	*like a name*
in the cracks & seams of our house,	*written*
they never retreat, don't question if it's life or grief	*on white stone—*
or a life of grief, a grain of sand, or one of their fallen,	*the word stumbling forth*
they crawl over the dead or carry back the dead.	*off the tongue*
The ants barely a grin on the kitchen threshold,	*from the back of the mouth*
colonies in ruined cake & doughnuts, uneaten comfort	*from the throat*
food left to harden, my father's miracle is turning bread to stone,	*from the gut*
his miracle is absolute negation, even cancer found him	*bubbling up from my*
an unsuitable host, though the radiation left him toothless,	*belief in nothing*
gumming forkfuls, sucking the juice from a morsel, pinching	*and everything, myself.*
the chewed-up ball from his lips & rolling it in his fingers,	*in poems like salt*
he's the beggar dog's all holy saint. Our family goes calmly	*that last an eternity*
about their business in lines, we file in & out, the clock	*on the face*
of our house, working steady the secondhand, & only	*there too you will find*
when he pulls the bread now stone from	*the charred remains*
the bag do the ants break from their spell;	*of words still*
they frenzy & touch each other tentatively	*trying to be spoken*
to know one another, to say the mission has ended,	*I hold my breath*
last night's platefuls of food scraped into the sink,	*like the earth*
their bodies electric with alarm & he sweeps them	*smothering a god*
into the runoff. He takes his time, why not be leisurely	*breathe*
about it, & breaks for the morning's first cigarette, pulls	*breathe*
his mouth to kiss & release smoke. He'll drink	*I sing*
to the single file of days: sugared black	*breathe*
in the stained coffee mug, & then crack	*breathe*
open the first bottle, the book with a dangerous title	*I stutter*

he'll read on the terrace in a wicker chair, the paint
peeling white flakes that fall at his feet in collapsing
layers, just like the laced prisms
that buckled beneath his fingertips
as he poked at the pillow of snow on the doorstep
of his childhood home, was it alive
that whiteness more air than body &
pushed aside at the day's end, no more
than a rag at the mouth of an empty cave.

this is not like singing
this is like penance
a dead boy is circled by ants
& my memory is shocked at itself
come let me add my measure
of salt to your white lips
running my hands over the hot
metal letters of your name
as the body of wind enters
like a stone
opening its mystery
this is how one finds his knees

Portrait of My Father X Days Before Dying

He has been dying for six years. The first cancer took hold in his throat, the tumor like a pit of amber, all the things left unsaid. Those who are of a religious persuasion would say he began dying the day he was born, he will soon be reborn; that tireless circle, fluff he would wave away, all that unseen/unproved business not for his engineer mind. In this life we need to first build, then inhabit, till its use runs out. My father is here in a photograph, exactly as I last saw him: in the leather recliner, his balding head the only thing not swallowed by a puffer jacket, the brick background of the fireplace, the fixture a joke of our Miami childhood home & the two times a year we set a fire: Christmas & New Year's. But he is cold every second of every day of what is left of his life. He has his eyes closed, swallowing that bite of whatever they've served him on that folding side-table where he keeps always within reach the TV remote, lighter & Marlboros, nail clipper & folded stack of paper towels—those he will use to spit out whatever he can't manage to gnash with his gums. Don't write of those things my mother will say. You cannot publish any of this until he's dead, she says. We have been trying to bridge the distance before that happens, but he goes further into silence, deeper into that down jacket. In this photo it is only his profile, stark shadow of cheekbone cut at a knife's edge, the perfect angle of his nose sloping from his wide forehead & his open mouth, bowing his head down, as if he cannot bear the weight of holding himself up any longer. His mouth open, a sad-eyed giant grouper in an aquarium wishing for the hook & the yank into the crushing sunlight. He balances a fork in his right hand, some unidentifiable morsel he forces himself to fake-eat for our sakes. How I saw him last time, backlit & smoking on the terrace, the silhouette of his curved back & hunched shoulders, already imagining that I'd remember exactly how he pulled on the cigarette like he was at the bottom of the abyss, that pull the deepest inhale, the tightest kiss of his lips, his fine fingers holding the cigarette tight & then the exhale of smoke rising stories above us, more things unsaid. He leaned forward & let out a fine stream of drool, & there was terror & beauty, all perfectly illuminated in his silhouette. I have to describe it in detail, though no one will want to read this, my mother assures. But in the photograph I now hold in my hand, behind my father is my mother's self-portrait on the mantle, strokes of Chinese ink, her long neck & bobbed hair looking away from my father, towards the window & the backyard that is surely dark, where they both sit & share cigarettes, the few words they trade back & forth about sleep & pains, & the things that are missing. My father handed me the list of these things in the form of a haiku— Need: // Beer // Cigarettes // Wine. That is what he needs, in his perfect handwriting, small pad of lined paper & blue ballpoint. It is clear, Father, what you need. Mornings you greet me with one word: coffee. No time for pleasantries; you wait in your chair, in this room that is not a living room, but a waiting room. There, in the bookshelves are the mystery novels, the detective novels, the war novels, all the books you've read in the waiting, rubbing your knees with expectation, for the tall figure to creak open the door & call your name. X days plus X days plus X days is the solution you cannot solve, cannot find X, you, my engineer father who filled pages with numbers trying to teach me while I muddied the page with tears. I could not understand all those numbers, that was your language, the things you were certain of, that you could prove, & for me those computations were spiderwebs, tangled & shredded by wind.

Concierto de Aranjuez

One day, people will line up to say:
I'm sorry about your father, unable to say *dying*
& so it'll sound like they lament his life,
their condolences for the being of him, my father
whom I knew very little about. Easy answer:
he loves Spanish guitar,
bife & berro from his Buenos Aires days,
—our father already bedridden,
toothless, down to one hundred pounds.
Before this, I looked for him in the mornings
when his head was still clear
& we drank coffee on the porch, his chile plants unwatered,
leaves buckling into themselves. It seemed there wasn't much
he wanted me to know about him.

Tonight, at the Aranjuez concert a young guitarist
plays the quiet regret of the adagio, his foot propped up on a little cot,
& his fingers curl around the neck of the guitar
& he plucks out sounds that tear chunks from my chest,
the cellos sawing deeper, the musicians holding their violins
like infants after a feeding.
I squeeze my husband's shoulder, this music also
playing through his own father's cancer.
The lives of these men &, in the mirror of us, their love rendered imprecise.
How memory sings in those empty spaces.

Earlier today we got news
my uncle died, my father's one friend at the end of the game.
The call came in as we walked through a garden of daffodils
& I quoted Wordsworth's lonely as a cloud
to my son, who then asked how a body becomes ashes.
We are both the living & the dead. How much
in the world & in our lives we have yet to notice. We kept walking
to the narcissus beds, & I told him
about a man who leaned over a pool

& could not tear himself away from his blooming,

or lose his reflection and disappear.

And yet, there are men who know how to humbly endure small deaths.

At the concert, the young guitarist makes a big show

between each movement; he gets up, bows

& exits stage left, but from my angle I can still see him

listening to the roar of the audience & each time—

three times—he repeats the same drama.

We all want him to return.

Even my son is transfixed, leaning over the balcony to see

the guitarist moving his fingers, but by the third time

I am tired of his grand exit & re-entry—how he salutes

the rest of the symphony & shakes hands

with the first-chair violin, then returns to his leather bench,

cradles the guitar & props his foot on the little sling.

I am ready

to never see him again & just live in the quiet

of the music that fills the room.

It is time

for the lights to come on, for the audience to file out

& for the hall to hold only silence.

What I know of my father, I've forgiven.

The Garden of Earthly Delights

He is imminent, they have told us, a softer way of saying
he is about to die, like the words *passed away*, passed
to a place that is far, not here, cannot or will not
say where. Passed, as if through a threshold, to a place
we cannot follow, unknown to us. *He died*. It has a thud
to it, a spade of soil, the two d's standing at either side
like bookends, *died*, bracing the solitary *i*, the self & the *e*,
his initial. His signature, a perfect birdswoop of wings.
      And taking him by the hand, he flexes his fingers in sleep,
as if strumming guitar strings, notes that resound
in the caves of Sacromonte, geraniums in clay pots.
A puzzle on the table, half completed, all that blue & green,
grass & sky, tiny naked bodies, towers of fleshy fruits, a carousel
of dancing animals, & from somewhere comes
the music of a guitar, notes played by an unseen hand.
The adagio echoes in that whitewashed cave as we watch him pass.

Hesperides

All this beauty cut down, all this sweetness
turning to rot, as we gather around
the pleather chairs in the funeral home's living room.
Flower arrangements mark the rectangular place,
center stage, where the coffin will be, while we greet
the early mourners, each pésame, pat on the back,
sympathetic nod, squeeze of the hand, adds one more
bloom to the dizzying smell. I catch my sons modeling
their navy suits in a mirror & I caution their preening.
Yes, you're handsome but don't linger. They stand next
to my husband & show off new graces, smiles & charm.
I love them for their lightness. My youngest daughter,
who's also taller than me, hovers like a shadow,
holds my hand, chin on my shoulder, & when it's too much,
bows her head, paints a half-moon on the silk
of my back. I bought their dark clothes,
I taught them how to respond when someone says I'm sorry.
And when their grandfather's coffin is wheeled in,
the scene is almost complete. Our family stands in line & I wonder
if we'll know when it's time to stop rehearsing.

III.

And Per Se And

In response to The Audre Lorde Questionnaire to Oneself

Not exactly infinity, our ampersand a stalled-out Mobius strip,
racecourse with an exit lane, highway with a runaway truck ramp,
twenty-seventh letter of the alphabet, Pompeian graffiti preserved by Vesuvius
from the first century AD. Ampersand melding of letters E, T,
ligature of my father E, my husband T's initials, one letter flows seamlessly
into the next; per se means *by itself*, now is slurred into the word we use today,
a mondegreen: ampersand. Handwritten, a crossed-out E, my dead father, plus
sign that gives equal credit, the math I still struggle to understand. Shorthand
of a former slave, Marcus Tullius Tiro, secretary of the Roman writer Cicero,
ampersand to show haste, experimentation, casualness, or dissent.
Ampersand as escudo: do not say *or*, do not say *but*, keep going in
a breathless run-on sentence, forever, list the ways I love you, all the ways
I am fire, glass. We will hold hands, lean in, just keep it coming,
we do not want silence, list the ways, point to the connections, give me more,
more, yes, you can come, yes, you too, all of you are invited,
we are in this together, a link, then another link. There are words
I do not have yet. Shapes of air, change made visible: cirrus, cumulus,
stratus, nimbus, the naming of clouds connects with each breath,
these words as prayer, to ask for forgiveness, to quell the fear
of eclipse, yes, isn't that me claiming space as a listener, to make
eye contact, to put my hand on your shoulder, to say,
I see you. So much of what we want is to leave a trace, but
also not to leave tracks, because when someone dies they take
who you were in their eyes; always the looking eyes of the moment
make me falter, I am gathering words, launching them
into the space outside us. Yes, I too am thrown back
by the waves, the idea sharking around the room that we have to act just right,
of how I need people, perhaps it's also hard to believe people need me,
Dueña de la razón, I need to take a step back, read the room, not just draw lines
around each other, not splinter or tremble, not stay in the periphery
as a fly wringing its hands. Yes, I promise I really am here, though in flux
like a swarm of insects, I've come to no static conclusion, though still I wonder
if these words are just glancing off an exoskeleton, I'm ready to bend,
to crack, to be that ampersand, here I am opening the door, I am ready
to hand it over, this heart I've bound into a figure eight & start again.

Ánima, Silueta de Cohetes: The Night I Met Him

After Ana Mendieta

1.

Flash powder lit hands up   she has
Set her body down   as seed & blossom
The match sparks the pulse   ignites
A record   of her simple presence   on earth
First sound   of pain   also   the first sound
Of pleasure   her curved hips   her torso incarnadine
In the flesh she has rendered it   on the ground   cut
Into mud   outlined   on wet sand   & now she is
Red orange yellow   & the hottest white
Black powder smoldering   hands up   she is
Rising in a column   of smoke   raised hands
In prizefighter gloves   belt-whip of stars   in the glory
Of a win   arms up   a gun   at her back
A trust fall   against the mountain's shoulders
Her entire body   exploding   take it   take it   all
Nothing   left to give she is
More   than smoke   more than   even the clouds

2.

Tequila drunk at a wedding / The night I met him / Dancing / The man who would be / My husband / Fireworks sizzling into water / That moment / I wanted to immolate / Myself no such / Happiness meant / For me / Not yet ready / For a man who could love / Me from all angles / No fear of deep water / Or sky / How it extends / In all possible directions / No walls to buttress / No safe corner / To peer out of / For me / There was only space / And space / Hours later alone / Laid out on a field of dew-wet grass / I played / For years / What it might be like / To disappear / From him / From me / Not unlike this / *Ánima, silueta* / Call her / Woman / Who is / Not there / And vividly marking / Her / Not being there

When We Were Long-Distance Lovers

At a farmers' market we buy speckled plums,
        peaches & persimmon to share.
After all these months apart we don't know
        how to hold each other's gaze, no words
to prove I deserve your return.
        As you lead me through side streets
to a lot overgrown with dandelions,
        the sun sinks behind a clump of mangroves
& I am that eye; I need to see to believe.
        We sit on the hood of my truck eating the fruits,
I let the juices dribble down my legs,
        your fingertip swirls the fallen nectar on my skin.
The sky strips to oranges & reds & means it;
        it's done with excuses.
All my life, I held back always a small part,
        small as a seed.
You eat a perfect circle around the peach, a halo,
        & offer half to me.
I take bites of sky. My teeth sink in,
        rattle over the pit.

Marginalia of *La Vita Nuova*

1.

At Dante's house I wander, disappointed
to find no wooden desk polished by constant touch, no letters
to friends written with a favorite pen, not even a lock of hair,
just white walls, legal documents & maps behind glass.

My only consolation at the giftshop: a postcard etching
of Paolo & Francesca, bodies intertwined,
his blond head plunging into her black tresses.

But I'm not thinking of the *Inferno*, rather, of the *Vita Nuova*.
Beatrice, a nine-year-old dressed in crimson,
crowned with idealizations, & in a dream,
forced to swallow Dante's burning heart.

And I am unsettled to think that this reminds me of you—
after three brief encounters & a few letters—
part of me wants to feed these illusions,
wants to be consumed.

I want to embrace this newness, but I am in Italy learning to be alone,
learning to shut down parts of myself,
already, they have grown quiet, have darkened.

Loss is not about emptiness,
but about a heaviness
that causes our heads to tilt into our hands.

2.

For two nights I've watched a man I pretended not to notice.
He reminds me of you—the languid sway
of his hips, each footstep a tug & release,

the heaviness of his stare, a darkness
like ashes surrounding light eyes.

I allowed him to pass
in the background of my vision,
afraid to look, afraid to see it was not you.

At the Piazza San Marco, pigeons swarm
on the arms & shoulders of children,
peals of laughter & fistfuls of corn,
smiles & cameras flashing, violins in crescendo,

I stand wishing for words to spark from my head,
a life made new by love, like the apostolic tongues
of flame converging at the golden cupola of the Basilica,
winged lions & angels blinding in the afternoon sun.

3.

On a street corner in Rome the flowerstands of agapanthus, gladiola & lily
beckon like exotic creatures, & I move to
photograph them, afraid they might run off but

after lowering the lens & taking a closer look,
I see they are fake—less life-like than love-like—
& I turn away, embarrassed.

At the Sistine Chapel, hordes of people point
& crane their necks like a mass UFO sighting,
Michelangelo's God suspended in blue—confident, precise—
with upraised palm, one swift stroke dividing
bodies between heaven & hell.

Beneath that barrel-vault blue, a blue that, sighing, asks,
What will it take for you to trust this new life?

Tin Anniversary

The plot concerns a man searching for his beloved. Today, as she stages
her portrait on a black sand beach, she thinks of the things she did
as a kid that could have killed her (red notebook number 28),
jumping off a bridge, drunk, into a canal at night; lights whirling,
bass throbbing & the cleft pill in her palm; notes of a favorite song,
tires shrieking to slam beneath an oak.
To her husband she promised newness & wonder but is distracted
daily: their youngest graffitties the couch with scowls, their second
born's laugh is a high kick, their eldest ponders as his spirit rises
to heaven, will it also have feet? At the back of what drawer
has she stuffed the will to keep those promises? It is there, somewhere,
she knows. She bites her fingers, grinds her cuspids blunt;
the day to day, it would be a relief not to have to do it. The ocean kneels
& rises, kneels & rises—he's proved it a decade's length:
queen of my heart & quick-draw apologies, a bowl of fresh whipped
cream. She promised on the water's edge, kneeling
& rising in a white dress, a circumstance where the less
possible something can be, the more it must be. She hears his voice
casting across the beach; what was it she promised? Hold on, hold on,
teetering on that fulcrum, the astonishing capacity to hold on.

Do You Know How Ugly You Are to Me Right Now?

It's that, sitting here, as you slice
the air with your assertive hand gestures over the folded
newspaper & sweating glass of orange juice & that I should
be listening to you in a stadium, the audience member of a self-help
speech—& yet I watch the horncurl of your hair spring up again
& again to emphasize words that I should add to my womanly checklist—
& I know you are staring at the purpled shadow of the weeks-old zit
on my chin, know you are dreading the downturned corners of my mouth
that remind you of my mother, & even as I nod consent, my eyes zero in
on the brown bit of frijoles stuck between your teeth; I imagine
you will smile in the mirror later & wonder how long it had been there.
Understand?, you ask. Yes, husband, I understand.
      At this moment we have lapsed
into the dark twist of the ribbon, that Mobius of love & hate, signature moves
once endearing now make us cringe, predictability marks a constancy,
once a groove, now a rut, & at this point we are just like my sisters, identical
twins who had the habit of lunging at each other: *I hate your face!*
Are we nothing without each other? Looped in that continuous echo,
in the beginning how we clung to one other, our heartbeats twinned,
now we search in the mirror of the other, unraveled, for all we yearn to love.

Hiking Through a Slot Canyon

There will be signs, they say, & now we expect it
at every corner, cannot admire the colored strata of rock,
the clouds above the crevasse of slot canyon,
the rays slanting in stagelights as we pass tight corners
to take off our packs, turn sideways, suck it in,
& inch through this birthcanal, this body of a snake,
& drop into the underworld.

We are not prepared,
hottest hour of the day, not enough water for two, let alone three;
my husband leads the way, my son buffered in the center & I follow,
anticipating a gasp, a cry, a bite at every turn.

And because pain is something
crouched beneath a rock, curled beneath an outcrop,
we walk in the sun expecting it, along this trench
once beneath the ocean, carved by currents through millennia.

There is a word for pain & a word for thirst,
but no specific term for our normal state. Not thirsty, not in pain.
At all turns: What are we dealing with—claws or talons,
serrated rows, incisors? One being swallows the next, a chain of mouths.

Pain could be a winged thing, a slithering thing,
a swishing fin, strike of fang or whip of tail. The bite we know to expect.
But do you ice it, or plunge the wound in boiling water?
Poison is ingested as a mushroom, but venom is injected.

Fear has to land somewhere, sink its hooks.
If it was awake, we would hear the rattling, they said.
We'd been warned about this one. How would we get around it?
Climb above it, arch hands & feet on opposite walls, bridge our bodies
over the danger, a snake cannot leap this high, how small is it?—
Will we be numbed or killed?

Then, white letters etched onto red wall,
in capitals: Watch out! & a drawing of a rattler
with a long arrow curving to its den beneath a ledge.
It was smaller & sleeping & we thought
we could tent our bodies over it, scoot across & over, hand/hand,
foot/foot, not disturb it or even alert it to our crossing,

but it was the waiting, the anticipation that whipped us into a frenzy—
how could we make it across without wanting to let go at some point,
cave in & fall into the pit?

        It lured us to fall, to consider that end,
& how that might also mean sleep & rest, finally an end.
And after much debate, we climb out & stand atop the plateau in the shade
of sagebrush & juniper, I pinch a berry & hold it to my nose,
the horizon frizzles into vapor.

        We look down into the striated chasm,
stone stacked atop stone, shrugging years, & we walk a broad circle
around the snake's lair, dip into the slot canyon further ahead
knowing there will not be any more signs from here on out,
& the snakes, real or imagined, will still be there.

Marriage as Tributary: What's Left in the Bend of May

If you ask me, water was the cure // why do we debate,

Spinning here on the brittle shell // of language, hot & hooded,

Does the desert taste its salt // do you detest me, leftover me

A trickle of love // we once mirrored.

If we split who am I // over & under our weave,

The facts dormant, acutely // I realize,

It's under, over // a frayed & hooked tributary

You are a creek at night that sounds // like an angel, shoreless.

Over, under, turn of the braid, shored, // I touch the ends

Of the earth in spite of the bind // we have held it

In the date of a calendar, // this world that will not offer

A bridge // but a landslide that will hold us

Down // we are a stone on the shore

Or rolling through the creek // was I that woman in the beginning,

What in the storm does float // a woman looking at the still

Crimson afternoon, // ransom in the rearview unmade for the leaving,

The sun a fruit, bitten into // & tossed aside,

Unknown angel, unwritten verb, // foreign star spinning on,

We are the waves & the grey shore // reaching across,

We rush // to fill that distance.

Bufo Lovesong

For my husband in El Salvador,
separated for eighty-three days
during COVID-19, 2020

Without you, the hours I measure in my skin,
deepening to a darker brown as I write
canalside. You say I worry too much,
& it's true, I often stay silent rather
than go off-key. Like the bufo frogs, I too,
find protection beneath a broad leaf, hidden
from the jaws of snake or iguana, invisible
to spear-beaked ibis. These days are wet sand
through my fingers, pouring out in hills & turrets.

Tonight, as I wade into the echoing loop
of throaty calls, I search for words to clap around
this music, what vessel it might pour it into, but
like the damp heat of Florida it unspools in all directions.
On the canal, the moon snags in the branches of an oak,
& the crickets click metallic & fall into silence as I pass.
The bullfrogs' bassnotes roll out in soft grunts, rise
to snores, another layer melds to a buzzy trill,
uniting in a wave & then shattering to solos, there
a piercing peep, there the throng
of a loose guitar string.

They do not sing for my enjoyment, though
I want to find pattern in their chants, not a chorus,
not even a song, but a claim they are ready
to mate, lay eggs, morph—to defend their reedy patch;
their froggy needs unconcerned by melody or harmony
or if their song announces the rains.
Each night you call from the other shore; I hold
the image of your face in my palm. Even now,

twenty years married, I still find myself
shy in the light of your gaze, at once inside
of me & outside, how it tests my worth; & at this hour
what I want is your voice & your hands to wrap
around me, the way the bullfrogs play their whole
bodies as instruments, breath thrumming vocal cords,
ballooning chests & lungs in reverberations.

Yours is a call that doesn't seek an echo
but an embrace, swelling & blooming, tracing
back to where one ends & the other begins.
It is because you call from that other shore
with all of your self that I can fling
my self into that darkness between notes.

Blank Card

After Magritte's The Tomb of the Wrestlers

Eyes in the roses you sent me, eyes in the roses you didn't send.
We are in the moment before the breath or after the breath, but not
The breath. // These flowers wink and breathe;
Their plush mouths touch everything unsaid, vowels roll
Round their mouths, fringed petals surround the pupil
That speaks for us: what is white, what is yellow,
What is red. // Our love said & unsaid: rose petals floating in a bath
Of herbs & holy water to wash off the year, fistfuls of gardenias torn
Off a shrub & flung onto the sidewalk, daisies tossed
Midair gathering on a carpet & trampled underfoot, plumeria
Threaded into a necklace or crown, the tendril's unfurling green,
And, other days, tulip buds wilting in a vase. // Years, all we planted
Pushed against soil & rose up. Was gathered, bound, wired & tied
With a ribbon, wrestled into a vessel. We tried our best. // Each day
The sun arcs across the sky, colors fade, smells wane, wrinkled
And brown, edges crimp, blooms limp & shatter in one breath. // Now,
The flowers' eyes are unblinking, a silence we wade into. Can we linger
Here, waist deep, lean back & float beneath these clouds? My lips open
To receive you. // The rose marks a before & after, grows large,
Then larger, petals push against four walls, bears down on the floor, spreads
Across the ceiling, until there are no more words, no room
For us now but this blossoming.

IV.

Stalemate

With lines from William Golding & Galway Kinnell

Knock the gamepieces off the board & begin again.

          Lay me down in the back of our Pontiac stationwagon

watch lights zoom up & away, we were astronauts

          with no identifiable mission, black holes

can be anywhere. Entropy, we collapse into self. Maybe

          there is a beast. Maybe it's only us. We did everything

adults would do. What went wrong? There's no stasis.

          What's most frightening about believing only in things

we can see? La fosa, the hole in the ground or gateway

          to another world we know nothing about? A rock skips

over the surface of a lake & what happens in the air

          if we find ourselves sailing through that air, touching

down on water, & taking off again, touching down again

          until the final plunge & descent. What do we know

about hope? How to dive in without causing a ripple?

          Does it depend on the object or what casts

that object? As if clinging could save us.

Caravana Migrante

Beyond this bridge, blue dust
clouds nestle their faces
into the collarbone of earth.
They trick us into thinking
they are mountains brooding
over downtown's buildings
checkered with darkness & light.
Evening weaves her hair
among the trees, her fingers
pull all color from the world.
Triangles of birds point
to directions we intuit.
Before us, only the long stretch
of road, & yellow street reflectors
guide our path. Breadcrumbs
our tires devour, leaving
no trace for the return.

Pentimento

*For Karla Turcios & the 1,218 Salvadoran women
listed as victims of disappearance, abductions,
or unexplained missing person cases in 2019.*

Take a hammer to it   **crush**
And put it back together   **slowly**
As if   you had to accept   the beating
Heat-maddened   **to taste**   what you meant to say
                The red mud   unpack that
Not all epiphanies   **the blossomed trees**
Softly lean   someone who is me & yet not me   & always with me
Let us now praise   **the birds**   or, as another alternative
That these actually exist in the world &   **are having**
        Their discussions: a curtain of air, puff of the drapes
        —spring   you sit & look at yourself from across the bed
Flick of the chin   **—the avalanche**, you, mirrored,
What are you looking at,   pockmark   **of sorrows settling**
        Trampled hoofmarks   **at last**   carried away,
            Their ground   a vapor, nothing to discover
        —and lovers   a blip on the map   & no one noticed [ ]
        Arriving in the park   you had to run from your cage
It isn't sadness   you had to howl   & bark   & tear at the ropes
That [ ] brings   & if it came at you with its lights on you had to stare it down
        Me here: you had to charge toward it, for the end
The bench   or beginning   of whatever was coming next
        Weathered   that hand   could've been anyone's hand
        With scars   there were things   you   had to chase after
    And peeling paint;   develop thorns, grow fangs, colors to attract or warn,
The grass grey   roots that charge deepest to find water
        With exhaustion   the trees puff their last flowers, then the seed
        I come to study bones of hope: backbreaking winds, months of drought
            Someone has etched a crucifix   someone who is not yet me
        Into the cracked skin of a tree   the ferns, quiet in the gutter
The flowers   their arms don't reach out
        Don't know   content just to exist   in their substrata

In their days drop by drop   **it's too soon**

  For their smiles, when it overbrims, but the eyes never

That rain you hold floods back, what feeds the ferns

  Still has a day survive & survive & not much else

To thunder you know look the other way

Along to its place, fingers in the wound

The white sigh the wounds glimmering, mumbling their blood

  Of night how to outlast

  Still desires each hit

  Its say a kind of buttressing, a hammering

The petal-cups is that all?

  Open a current of air lifting a curtain, a soft gush,

As if that hand could've been anyone's hand

To the first hint one thing eats the other to stay alive

  Of a kiss the way it goes unnoticed

And I am singing in its familiarity

As if a polished truth, a tooth

With the first fractured & the tongue returns

  Bruised to find the broken edge there

  Mouth & there & there

Bold letters are Andrés Montoya's "Crush."

70

Hermitage

Say there is an animal surfacing.
Say it is a fin or a mouth.
          Hunger seeps between the rocks.
Say there is a haze caulking tree limbs to cloud.
          I am fed by silence.
The neighbor's face rises above the fence
          But when I call, he does not respond.
I would like to think I do not need anyone.
I drift above the palms, pen in hand,
          While a leashed animal snuffles at my feet.
The neighbor's path descends to black sand,
          The ocean's silk cut with lace.
Say the animal hides behind me, a shadow.
          The waves throw up their arms.
Who am I to say this seawall will resist.
Who is to say I am not waving a white flag.
          The animal tunnels the ground.
The vertices of two vultures form a cross.

To My Reflection as I Wash Dishes

That's not a good angle, I say. Everything is a backdrop
begging for a woman to pose. But those days are behind us,
we're not the virgin, not the holy mother. That uniform has faded.
Re-dye the mantle. Tear the gown's seams. Re-do until all is a taut cloth.
No, my dear, we are an unmade bed and these plastic gloves—
you paid extra for the pink. And we know blood only washes out
under cold water. You pretend you still believe, but the blood
has staggered and the music is closing in. Now the bark peels easily
from the pine. Tinder for the pyre. Here, your head crowned in morning light,
no songs for regret or pain or shame. I have woven thorns into my hair.
Those quarter-moon ideas shook the tree, and shook the tree and it bent
and gave its leaves, but offered no fruit. And I feel thirsty.
My circling has kicked up dust. Some days it's nothing more than a hum,
sometimes it's the sound of water gurgling into a sink. The body wants
to exist among these things. Popular science says humming
is the archetype of love. The needles of the pines whoosh in the wind.
It ends in an out breath. And I'm not comparing myself to this backyard tree
that claws dirt, throws down root fingers. We all want to be held up
and know that someone will be calling soon, that someone will take
our photograph and share it. You know it's incomplete without the photo.
Am I this afraid of vanishing? Go for the deep stare. Pose.
All that transcends, remains. The word "Still" as a title.
Will I leave a trace is not a question I'm asking because
the pleasure was there to be had. But true things necessarily sting.
You did the woman's part. Now you take up space.
Remember, once, I was stuck in an elevator with four men and after an hour,
clamoring for fresh air, I climbed to the topmost of the moving boxes.
I looked down from my tower and one of the men said, *Don't worry*
we won't do anything to you. Every story is an animal devouring itself.
Talk to me about a world where women are their own saviors.
We value being fruitful (not rotten, not barren) and we offer the best piece
to others, face problems by working harder. You set the direction,
speed of the spin, tilt of axis. You were holding a long rope,
no longer a long rope because yesterday at the MRI, your body

was in the intimacy of the machine where the unseen, unobserved
is what's dangerous. My mother taught me not to say I love you
as a goodbye because she considered it wasteful to scatter words
better saved for special occasions. Love yourself, she'd say,
as she combed my hair and pulled it into a rope braid and here I am
still trying to mumble those words to this face of mine.

Vanitas

Pain refuses
    to be ornamental;
        the rest, a vapor.
The onion peels to the center—
          root or nothing
    but an empty pocket.
Because the Lord promises victory
    to the surrendered
        believer.
Remind me again
    what happened:
        search for the wounded
    to rescue, let
        their hooks sink
          into me, and deny
    the urge to kick
        them off.
I like the taste
    of blood, songs
        with mournful vowels,
    the body's animal needs.
Drag me back,
    to fullness, then
        over-touched.
I am at the last rung
    and the ladder
extends no further.

Five American Sentences

To prove to an unseen someone, a future self, that I am enough.

A loved one drowning, just out of hands' reach; hover your hand above a flame.

That person is gone from this earth, what we could've evolved to is finished.

You are now in this world without his esteem, untethered, the string snapped.

I too, someday, will end, & this forgetting is a kind of freedom.

Verano, El Repunte

After Pájaros, Cementerio
de Graciela Iturbide

We slept in fog.
      Our lives pressed between two panes.
I've taken an ax to all that's browned.
Set the palm roof onto the pyre.
      The braid unbound.
I pulled the pearl buttons from your shirts.
      Made eyes for cotton dolls.
I hate the retelling of dreams.
      I carry out the last that will burn.
Birds double as smoke, cloak us with ash.
      On the doorframe, a caterpillar shroud.
      I am no taller than these walls.
All that is flammable at the forefront.
How do you end if not an epiphany?
      Wings glance my skin.
My hands empty of what I still want.

What My Father Taught Me About Time Travel

I want to need to repeat you again
& you need to leave
so emptied you cannot fill
the bowl-headed sky, the antiseptic clouds
burning white. I'm playing with
a cat's dead bird—who knows
what skull & crossbones I can
release to this world.
I can feel the quivering of your body,
the heaviness I'm causing. I want to leave
& so you leave, feet buried in the sand, head in hands,
unrecognizable statue. The sea unfolds &
the sky moves closer. We stand exposed
like lightning rods, then glass.

The Art Is Knowing When to Stop

Untouched, a rock is a rock.
                    Hold it in your hand & it becomes stone.
When the sculptor sees the sculpture in the stone,
                    it becomes art.
Turner's *The Fighting Temeraire*, painted at the height
                    of his career, is said to be a self-portrait.
The sun goes down on the British Empire,
                    end of an era, the grand warship tugged into the Thames
to be chopped up & sold for scraps.
                    It's the mystery we glorify.
The Mayan stelae I thought so wise,
                    so deep, but was really a billboard claiming:
Warrior King 28 Rabbit killed five hundred soldiers on this spot.
                    Or in Burma, the temple decorated with curving
calligraphy in translation said, the Win family
                    donated these ten bricks.
An outline of footprints on wet sand points
                    back at the absent creator.
In my self-portrait I would not be a tree,
                    roots pushing asphalt, bowing beneath
powerlines. I would not be a tree mid-field among
                    the slow mouths of moon-eyed cows. Nor a backyard tree
heavy with fruit, rising stories above a woman who pulls up
                    her shirt to make a basket, while her son climbs up
to the highest branches & tosses down jocotes to her.
                    Not the tree, not the fruit, but the seed, hard as a rock.

I am grateful to the editors and coordinators of the following literary spaces in which versions of these poems first appeared:

"Videofeed from the American Embassy in El Salvador," *BOMB Magazine*, Summer 2022.

"Cavities Are Inherited," *West Trestle Review*, May 2021.

"Caracol," *The Shallow Ends*, May 2020.

"What My Father Taught Me About Black Holes," and "Probably the Most My Father Has Ever Said to Me," *South Florida Poetry Journal*, May 2020.

"Concierto de Aranjuez," *DIALOGIST*, November 2022.

"Escape Room" and "Portrait of My Father X Days Before Dying," *Diode Poetry Journal*, August 2022.

"Caravana Migrante," *Esferas*, New York University, Department of Spanish and Portuguese, December 2021.

"Blank Card," *SWWIM Every Day*, February 2021.

"Hacer de Tripas Corazón," and "What My Father Taught Me About Time Travel," *Los Angeles Review*, September 2021.

"To My Reflection as I Wash Dishes," *Womanish* art exhibit, Wynwood, Florida, 2021—ongoing.

Spanish translations of "Relinquenda," "Hija, an Inheritance," "I Prided Myself on Being Aguantadora," and "Mamá Tacuazín" are included in *Piedra*, a chapbook published by La Chifurnia, El Salvador, 2022.

"What My Father Taught Me About Evolution" and "The Art Is Knowing When to Stop," *Five Dials*, Spring 2022.

English versions and Spanish translations of "El Puente" and "Invasive," *Revista El Pez Soluble*, June 2022.

NOTES

The phrasing of "Relinquenda" is inspired by Joanna Rawson.

"The Giantess" borrows language from Tracy K. Smith's "Bright" & "The Machinery of Evening."

The carpentry images in "How to Crack an Egg" are inspired by Yusef Komunyakaa.

"Hacer de Tripas Corazón" includes lines from Rainer Maria Rilke's *Duino Elegies* & Joy Harjo's *Conflict Resolution for Holy Beings*.

"What My Father Taught Me About Evolution" responds to the work "amor," 2016, by Efraín Caravantes. Gracias por tu amistad.

The spider image in "The Hero Myth" is inspired by Tommy Orange's *There There*.

The right-hand column of "Turning the Stone, Contrapuntal" includes lines from Andrés Montoya's poems in *A Jury of Trees*, mainly from "Generation" as well as "Lorena's Whisper," "Tree," and others.

"The Garden of Earthly Delights" responds to the central panel of the triptych by Hieronymus Bosch.

"Ánima, Silueta de Cohetes: The Night I Met Him" resulted from an ecphrastic project with Emma Trelles.

"Tin Anniversary" responds to the work of Robert Sapolsky, American neuroendocrinology researcher and author.

"Hiking Through a Slot Canyon" includes a line from *Loneliness* by John T. Cacioppo, cofounder of the field of social neuroscience.

"Stalemate" includes two lines from William Golding's *Lord of the Flies* and one line from Galway Kinnell's "Little Sleep's-Head Sprouting Hair in the Moonlight."

"Pentimento" is built around the poem "Crush" by Andrés Montoya. Montoya's words are in bold typeface. *Pentimento* (Italian for *repentance*) is an alteration in a painting evidenced by traces of brushstrokes on previous layers that reflect how the artist has made changes in the composition throughout the process of painting. This poem was written during my Letras Latinas DC Ekphrastic Residency and responds to the exhibit *Frédéric Bazille and the Birth of Impressionism*, specifically "Study for a Young Male Nude." For more info, go to https://www.nga.gov/features/bazille-hidden -compositions.html.

"To My Reflection as I Wash Dishes" responds to the exhibit "Selfish" from *Womanish*, Wynwood, Florida.

"Five American Sentences," after Allen Ginsberg, and with thanks to Jen Karetnick for the prompt.

"What My Father Taught Me About Time Travel" is what it is because of Christopher Soto's editing. Gracias por esas rondas de boxeo.

"The Art Is Knowing When to Stop" responds to a conversation with artists Baltazar Portillo and Amber Rose, and my dear friend Julian Altamirano.

SPECIAL THANKS

I first encountered the word *relinquenda* in one of my mother's journals. She held it as a motto and I adopted it as my own. I wrote this book during the first months of 2020, immediately after my father's death, and while I was stranded in Miami during the first wave of the COVID-19 pandemic; the borders of El Salvador were closed and so I was separated from my husband and children and living with my mother, grandmother, and aunt. Although I formulated the words for years, I mined these poems from three journals and wrote drafts on my grandmother's terrace that looks out to her garden.

Throughout the course of two years our family lost various members of our elder generation, my father-in-law, my mother's brother and sister, and others, culminating with the death of my maternal grandmother in November 2021. For me, this book was about learning resilience, taking example from my father's stoicism and endurance. I thought I knew something about loss and letting go, but on January 1, 2022, my mother died of a heart attack and I was shattered. Our lives were enmeshed. This will be my greatest act of relinquenda: living without my mother. And so, I dedicate this book to her, as I dedicate to her every poem I've ever written, and every poem I will ever write. For Violeta, always.

All my love to everyone that has supported me and my work: my family, especially my husband, Tomás, allí, en tus manos está mi corazón; my children: Maya, Javier, Sebastián; my brother and sisters: María Elena, Eduardo (and honorary sister, Jess), Valeria, and Adrianna; the matriarchs of the family: Tía Marcia and María Marta; my tías Marta Silvia and Carolina, and my extended family. Thank you for believing in me.

Eternal thanks to my dear friends and first readers: Christopher Soto, Emma Trelles, Efraín Caravantes (por las traducciones también), Lucía de Sola, Leo Boix (y por la colaboración), Francisco Aragón—gracias, gracias for your insight and generosity; and thanks to Lisa Fay Coutley for your valuable feedback. For those long, inspiring conversations with the Miami Poetas Collective: Caridad Moro-Gronlier, Catherine Prescott (special thanks to Om Shala), Elisa Albo, Jen Karetnick, Mary Block, Mia

Leonin, and Rita Martinez—thank you for your wisdom and cariño. Many thanks and much love to the CantoMundo familia. To my hermanas del alma who've cried and laughed with me: Mayita, María Marta, Minina, Mónica, Ana Gloria, Gloria, Tere, Maria Elena, Caro, Paola, Matia, Anna, Vero, Bárbara, Fermina, María José, Carolina, Marta, Leo, Lianne, Becky, Amy, Suzie, Traci, Lisa, Brenda . . . there are so many more than can be named here. That light is you.

Todo mi gratitud para Jorge Galán, Tania Pleitez, Miguel Huezo Mixco, Elena Salamanca, Alberto López Serrano, Muriel Hasbun, Miroslava Rosales, Otoniel Guevara, y Josue Andrés Moz por su apoyo y por su asesoría con las traducciones de mis poemas. Traducir mi obra ha sido una parte esencial en mi proceso de edición. Gracias por sus ojos y por su generosidad.

My wholehearted gratitude to Reginald Dwayne Betts for connecting with my work and selecting my manuscript. Thank you for seeing me.

I am infinitely grateful to the National Poetry Series donors and sponsors, founders and directors, and to coordinator Beth Dial for making this book possible; it is a life-changing gift.

Special thanks to Beacon Press: Helene Atwan, Beth Collins, Melissa Nasson, Susan Lumenello, Haley Lynch, Priyanka Ray, and the entire team for your support, appreciation, and careful attention to my work.

My hand-on-heart to the readers of this book and to those who've suffered a loss. Como decía mi mamá: Take time to love yourself. I'm tending the flowers, keeping the candle lit. Les abrazo.

ABOUT THE AUTHOR

ALEXANDRA LYTTON REGALADO is the author, editor, or translator of more than fifteen Central America–themed books. She is also the cofounder and codirector of Editorial Kalina. Her debut poetry collection, *Matria*, won the St. Lawrence Book Award, and she is a CantoMundo fellow and a winner of the Coniston Prize. She holds an MFA in poetry from Florida International University and an MFA in fiction from Pacific  University. Her work has been published by the Academy of American Poets and has appeared in *The Best American Poetry*, *Narrative*, *Gulf Coast*, and *Creative Nonfiction*, among others. Lytton Regalado works as an advocate for contemporary Salvadoran artists as a member of the board of directors of MARTE, the Museum of Art of El Salvador. She currently splits her time between San Salvador and Miami, where she lives with her husband and three children.

LUCY TOMASINO